REVERBERATIONS

REVERBERATIONS

COLLAGE OF DREAMS

STANIA J. SLAHOR

iUniverse, Inc.
Bloomington

reverberations
collage of dreams

iUniverse books may be ordered through booksellers or by contacting:

iUniverse
1663 Liberty Drive
Bloomington, IN 47403
www.iuniverse.com
1-800-Authors (1-800-288-4677)

ISBN: 978-1-4759-5210-0 (sc)
ISBN: 978-1-4759-5212-4 (hc)
ISBN: 978-1-4759-5211-7 (ebk)

Library of Congress Control Number: 2012918472

Printed in the United States of America

iUniverse rev. date: 11/05/2012

to Ludovit—
without him my poems
would never flourish . . .

CONTENTS

ILLUSTRATIONS BY JANA TRNKA

INTRODUCTION

Motto:
A book must be the ax for a frozen sea inside us.

Franz Kafka

Born in Bohemia, now part of Czech Republic, I frequently visited Prague, Franz Kafka's birthplace, and would tour through historical regions of the city till my feet on the cobblestone pavement began to hurt. My homeland with its past, beauty, culture and destiny, had a great influence upon my early creativity and writing. But after the Russian occupation in 1968, my family found a second home in Canada where new circumstances affected largely my poetry.

All my observations and experiences in *'Reverberations'* elicit my emotional reactions in the presence as in *'Metamorphosis'* and *'Bewitched by sea'*. Other poems disclose what happened in my unquiet past as described in the ballad *'Boy and the rose'*, or in the enigmatic remembrance *'Mystery of beads'*. Sometimes, they are just playful as in *'Speaking nature'*, or *'The afternoon of a faun'*, reverberating with imagination and fantasy.

The rhythmical sounds can cause increasing tension and echoes. The entire title 'Reverberations' resounds with dreams, intuitive cognition, pleasures and sorrows. In opposition to the injustice as in *'Mountblanc fountain pen'* and in *'Monument'*, I take a stand against a ruling authority, and emphasize my protest about the deception and oppression in my large-as-life world.

Several poems in *'Reverberations'* were written during vacations with my husband Ludovit in Progreso, a fishing village in the Yucatan. Every winter, we rent a beach house on the Gulf of Mexico, and enjoy the company of Mayas, and the sea, under the world's highest sky.

It was there, that many of my poems were inspired and composed. For example, '*A nautical dream*' was written under the influence of the lonely sight of discarded boats on deserted shores. A poem, '*Where the one-winged angels dart*', pictures my fascination with a daring team of sailors, racing against the wind on a rough sea.

Some poems were written while travelling across the mountains and prairies or along the great lakes of my home province of Ontario.

Our frequent returns to Europe bring us back to our youth and experiences, refresh our memories and reignite friendships. But we are always glad to come home to Canada, the land we have grown to sincerely love.

2012   Stania J Slahor

Acknowledgement

Publishing a poetry at my old age, seems to be quite rare. Nevertheless, my ideas cannot lay fallow because by writing the poems, my life seems to be fulfilled.

I owe a deep debt of gratitude to my editor and friend, Joan Matchett. I always trusted her literary experience and skill. She patiently edits all my poetry without aborting any of my strange ideas. I appreciate her help in finding right idioms to express images in my acquired language.

My thanks go to the performance poet and playwright, Penn Kemp, for her final editing. As an experienced reader of my poems she never crosses out some inapplicable expression, but makes a gentle note of it in the margin. After all is done, we celebrate.

I want to acknowledge my friend, and literary expert from Chapters Indigo, Diane Ryan. She never fails to ask me for my new poems. I respect her ideas and appreciate her opinions and understanding.

Many thanks go to my other readers, whose love of poetry is in their blood: to Vladimir Kopecky, Brooks & Elinor Rapley, Carlos Argaez, Landy Cardenas, Yanny Jimenez, Joyce McInerney, Lee Siebert, Magdalena Krondl, Libuse Snepp, Lorraine Alquire, Helena Slavik, Zdenek Zidek, G.R. Ganapathy, Vladimir and Jana Privratsky, and to everybody who likes to read my poems.

Some of them are from the Yucatan, and know very little English. Still, they cherish my writing and comprehend it with their open hearts. During each winter, their unique peninsula, fellow Mayans, the sea and sky, instill an endless inspiration and love in my soul. Gracias, amigos!

I acknowledge my stepdaughter, the renown European artist, Jana Trnka. With her talent and individual spirit, she illustrated all three books of my poetry. Her magical images interconnect with the underlying pattern of my ideas and her superb designs of the covers are wonderful pieces of art.

My gratitude goes to a rest of my family, especially to Jiri, Zdenka and Martin, also to Lisa, Gautier and Maggie, who lovingly bear my moods of joys, sorrows, success and doubts. Without their encouragement and online help, my work would be less eager and open. Thank you.

I sincerely acknowledge my husband Ludovit, who is my inspiration, friend and jewel of my heart. His intelligence, knowledge of nature, of people and life are very important for my understanding of the world. We live in our little universe, which we have created together through our love and pains. Without him, I would be lost, and spent, and none of my poems would flourish.

Stania J. Slahor

EDITOR'S NOTE

Stania's poetry stems from her troubled heart.

Filled with memories of partings and loss she finds solace in the rhythms of the sea and stars and through their imagery expresses the joys and sorrows of her life. Hers is a universal story hidden in verse.

Our friendship began on a Mayan beach and developed over the years into a fusion of souls.

Stania is a thought-provoking artist and poet who encourages her readers to cherish their dreams. As her editor, I help her find the words and images to express her ideas and memories in her adopted language.

Joan Matchett

I

eternal presence

Motto:

"Beauty is a reversion to the pre-divine lingering in man as a memory of something that existed before his presence . . . prior to the Gods."

Hermann Broch

Motto:

"I feel more and more every day, as my imaginations strengthen, that I do not live in this world alone but in thousands worlds."

John Keith (letter Oct. 18, 1818)

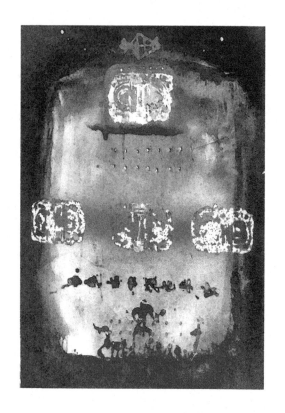

Jana Trnka, 'Imagination'

metamorphosis

strolling on the beach
revives my memory
of being at one
with the ocean

a polished pebble
flung upon the shore
by the violent surge
of a storm

the miniature flicker
of a silver fish
tossed
from tinselled roulette
of a whirling school

a wide-winged pelican
shooting across
quiescent sky
in a synchronized squad
searching for prey

a pure
effervescent pearl grown
in a twilight cache
on a spiral staircase
of an oyster shell

a slow-floating isle
of sea-grass
coaxed
from a coral meadow
by the tide

time and again
destroyed
in hostile discord
yet repeatedly revived
in the ocean's womb
to embryonic life

*   *   *

bewitched by sea

the passionate sea
whispers its secret
to basking waves
reposing lazily
upon the surface

with the setting sun
the azure expanse
suddenly changes
to an immense caldron
of molten gold
from the solar mine

the truculent sky cloaks
a low-burning horizon with
tattered drapes
thoroughly drenched
in a fathomless well

a capricious wind
ripples the surface
and white-crested waves
pursued by blistery clouds
heavy with rain
anxiously jump
in panic

on a roofed patio
of an abandoned beach-house
an invisible man
finds his refuge
in a creaking
rocking chair

and all night long
back and forth
vigorously rocks
bewitched
by the moan
of the crying storm

*   *   *

Jana Trnka, *"A nautical dream"*

a nautical dream

there is a score of ships
abandoned
and torn into tatters
on a remote shore

but the wounded vessels
dream of
faraway journeys
across the ocean
from one port to another
not to be wrecked
anymore

they lay ruined
buried for years
in dunes
but all at once
their hardy spirit
revives new courage
for further ventures

they dream
of sailing with
favourable winds
wafting them safely
to unknown harbors
afar

*   *   *

lagoon

from yucatan

in mid february
a nearby lagoon
abruptly lost
its vividness and shine

for many moons
before
a large group of flamingos
flew above
its surface

some waded
knee-deep in the shoal
craning beaks
for abundant food

their rosy reflections
playfully shimmered
and quietly rose
to the open space

but surprisingly
one morning
a large
pink cloud of
gaggling birds
attracted by the moon
soared
into the sky
heading
to a distant lagoon
a promise of plenty

disappointed
by the emptiness
i noticed
a lonely flamingo
standing
on one leg
beside the verge

a broken statue
of shattered glass
perhaps too old
or ill to fly
to the end
of his journey

*   *   *

white shores of paradise

like a snake
furtively crawling on
a winding course
along the bay
the boisterous tide
licks
the vacant strand
tangled with
seaweed
and fragmented shells

undulating waves
roll
with a plaintive howl
onto the shore
and happily lapping
flow back
reduced to silence

there are black ravens
frightful devils
soaring in circles
in the sky
abruptly rising
vanishing blank
into a misty height

the astounding seaside
captures
spry mind

that one may live
and some day die
transcended
by the promise
of paradise

*   *   *

Jana Trnka, "Surfing"

where the one-winged angels dart

unbridled sky
mirrors her face
in the eyes
of the truculent sea

approaching
from a harbour
the adventurous team
of one-winged angels
gathers full speed
racing
with the wind
on tempestuous waves

their translucent sails
like flattering wings
of dragonflies
attract an echelon
of pelicans
gyrating rapidly
in ritual spin

once in a while
one of the sailors
topples briefly
to the swelled surface
capsized
by a gust

but emerging fast
from the plunge
the dauntless surfer
darts
through the air
and elated
by the salt-kisses
of seductive waves
lusts for freedom
ravishes the pleasure
of heedless flight

*   *   *

poetic puzzle

boning a head
of a soft-cooked fish
i pilfer its tongue
as a special delicacy
for fastidious taste

but as i savour it
daintily
with epicurean greed
an alarming idea
flashes across
my mind

will i become mute?

why do
the sweet-toothed italians
—the fervent lovers
of delicate
nightingale tongues—
used to have voices
like angelic cherubs
burst into songs?

*   *   *

evoked by the sea

the sea teaches patience
by tyrannical wrath

its timeless beauty
and power
rise
to a seventh heaven
upon the sky

like a spumous wave
shattered by the blow
of a cliff
into a million
miniature suns
i feel
i am flying
in tiny pieces
of imagination
into nothingness

*   *   *

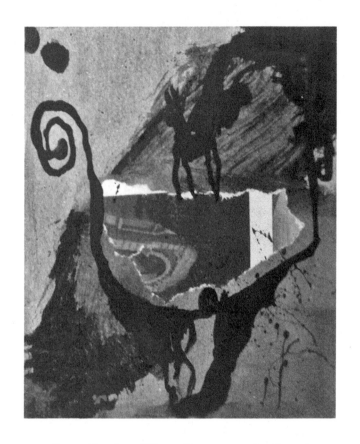

Jana Trnka, "The afternoon of a faun"

the afternoon of a faun

browsing
in fresh hoof-traces
on a sandy beach
of costa blanca
i caught sight
of a mythical faun
running in pursuit after
a pretty nymph
flirting
and insubstantial
as air

but from afar
the rhythmical clacking
of a brisk gallop
revealed
the silhouette of
a solitary stranger
riding on horseback
through a gold passage
paved
by the setting sun

*   *   *

where the sea and sky come together

where the sea
and sky come
together
they coalesce
integrate wistfully
to make love

the trembling ripples
of running waves
indulge
and celebrate
the new day
endowed
with prismatic colours
of dawn

*   *   *

Jana Trnka, "Pigeons"

a child chasing pigeons

a noisy crowd
of carnival goers
gathered
at a crumbling
bus station
in a busy
mexican city

unafraid
two greyish pigeons
fly down from
a nearby tower
and a little
mayan girl
claps her hands
to chase
the puffing birds
around
the station yard

creating laughter
and disarray
the trio
darts
among the crowd
causing chaos
in the traffic

occasionally
an alarmed pigeon
takes a wing
circles over
an area
then soft-lands
on the ground
to run and coo
beside the giggling child

unmindful of time

*   *   *

the road of a stranded whale

our rough drive
on a battered highway
resembles the call
of a stranded whale
imprisoned below
cracked asphalt
haunted
by memory
of submarine life

the homesick cry
under our wheels
whistled
by the beluga
to a distant sea
fills us with anguish

halted
by construction
in a motionless car
we anticipate
a utopian design
for future roads

the bumpy surface
of the highway
would be coated
interlaced with layers
of parallel grooves

much like
phonograph records
of old
that would produce
agreeable
musical sounds
to entertain passengers
during the drive

*　　*　　*

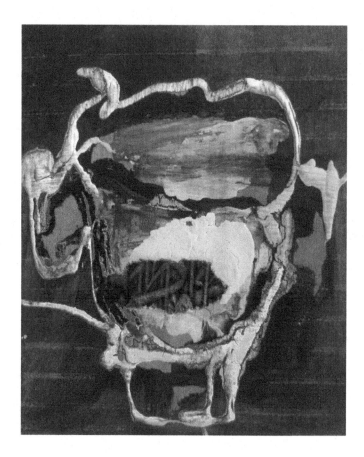

Jana Trnka, "Footlights"

footlights

a spectacular sundown
performed on the floor
of countryside
is framed
by claret curtains
and glinting footlights
to illuminate
the evening

a volatile moon
tiptoes slowly across
the paling sky
reaches for roofs
humped with
dilapidated chimneys
and curiously peeps through
rickety-tipsy fences

a dazzled audience
watches her sift
through a milky sieve
the constellations
of the zodiac

to end the show

*   *   *

magical nights

i will never forget
our hand-in-hand walks
during late
tropical nights
along a colonnade
of arching palms

we crossed the garden
littered with ripe
coconut globes
and after
closing the gate
turned back in steps
of moonstruck shades
on the path

astonished
we quietly listened
to voices
of scintillating stars
singing
in unison
over our heads

*   *   *

suicide of iguanas

death is uncanny
apocalyptic
killing
with the bravura
of a mad conductor

a heart-rending
tv report
from florida about
the unprecedented
cold winter
recounts
the suicidal behaviour
of the green
dragon-iguanas
causing great despair
to enthusiasts of nature

the upsetting video
calls to mind
unfortunate people
with incurable illnesses
without hope
of putting an end
to their suffering
and pain

unfortunately
the alarming news
does not explain
the iguanas' mistrust
that warm sunshine
will return
to quicken
the deadly slow
circulation
of their freezing blood
and bring them
back to life

*   *   *

the legends of time

the legends of time
engraved in rocks
of primeval mountains
shield
the dormant memories
of forgotten events

to unearth
their secrets
we rely upon myths
that tell of catastrophes
of the biblical deluge
sent by the deities
in retribution
to annihilate
civilizations
in the earthly past

*   *   *

II

speaking nature

Motto:

"A lake . . . is earth's eye; looking into which the beholder measures the depth of his own nature. The fluviatile trees next to the shore are the slender eyelashes which fringe it, and the wooded hills and cliffs around are its overhanging brows."

Henry Thoreau

Jana Trnka, "Speaking nature"

speaking nature

as an intrepid child
i understood
the ingenious language
spoken by plants
birds
fishes
snakes and boulders
—my intimate friends

their musical voices
resounded
from the air
treetops
babbled in creeks
over pebbles
from cascading falls

signalled
by butterfly's wings
always speaking clearly
to the child's heart
i wish
never to have lost

*   *   *

an upside down world

sheaving crisp armfuls
of freshly cut wheat
on the ripened field
of my youth
i discovered that
the world
looked different
even more magical
when watched
from upside down

bowed
to bristly stubble
i admired
the glamour
of topsy-turvy countryside
basking
in the sunshine
between my straddled legs

*   *   *

books and the cat

for diane

my favourite bookstore
in an old region
of the city
a little planet where
i can be deliriously lost
contemplating
how to nurture
the fragrant
thorny rose
rooted in my soul

the manager
recognizes me
and with her salespeople
who know
and love the books
on the shelves
assists to me
pick several copies
to sample

encased
in a reading-chair
in a quiet alcove
i begin to turn over
the freshly printed leaves
and concealed
from the busyness
of the outside world
i silently listen
to a whir
in my reader's heart

ready to leave
i stroke
the manager's
remarkable cat
stretched lazily at
the cash-register
among
randomly piled cards
books on display
a filigree vase
with a small nosegay
of dry flowers

my friendly attention
causes the animal
to protract
and purr
while surveying me
insolently
with her enigmatic
jade eyes

the open windows
to a cat's soul

i pay
and with a new book
in a shopping bag
leave
my familiar store

anxious to read

*   *   *

a miracle on the parched field

in july
the fields
became cracked
stone-dry
wilted

acres of beans
planted in spring
lost their moisture
and withered
our hopes of
redeeming debts

for several weeks
of hot weather
we waited
for a miracle of rain

whenever
the cumulative clouds
darkened in the distance
they moved away
or evaporated
into sky

frustrated we kneeled
in a parched bare corner
of a suffering field
and quietly begged
the god
to take
a pity on us
amen

all of a sudden
without a warning
precious drops of rain
fell on thirsty soil
healing
cracked wounds
our hopes
and pain

*   *   *

playing with raindrops

my mother said
that i can walk
between the raindrops
and never get wet

how have i learned?

just close an umbrella
and recklessly stroll
playing with raindrops

my rainproof game

*   *   *

Jana Trnka, "Reverberations"

reverberations

dragging my bike
up the steep road
bordered with
telephone poles
transfigured
into a puzzle

as i approached
several wooden posts
i heard
some sustained
reverberations
gradually rise
and eventually
fade out
as i passed

but at a closer distance
i noticed a volume
of puzzling sounds
came to be lauder

astonished
i put my ear
onto a weathered pole
to find out
the cause
of this strange
phenomenon

by surprise
i have heard
barely audible
distant sounds
of human voices

some speaking
laughing
arguing
and swearing
from town to town
on the extended
telephone line

*   *   *

a touchstone

a handful of stones
in my pocket
surprises me
how warm
nearly alive
they feel

above all i cherish
my touchstone
a small piece
of granite
found by my boyfriend
years ago
on our lone stroll

when i hold it
in my palm
i could hear
my infatuated heartbeats
for the old lad
i still madly love

*   *   *

temptation

a lovesong

embrace
and pass to me a sun
incandescent
red-hot
radiant
never setting down

embrace
and imprison me
in your arms
by lovesick whispers
intimate tales
of the thousand
and one nights

*   *   *

inseparable shadow

with my twin shadow
we are an odd
inseparable couple

whether in motion
idling
faint
or dark
my fellow-double
follows at my heels
displaying my shades
over the walls
under my skirt
on the flat floor

but when darkness falls
without much pity
or saying good-byes
he vanishes
nonchalantly
for the night

agitated
i bend out
from the balcony
finding him fading
on the curb

but as i move away
he climbs
on all fours
behind me

into the house
living
in mutual concord
for life

*   *   *

moving the mountains

there is a mystery
about the dream

like a ball
of finely spun yarn
it lingers
in the past
rolls to the present
unveils private secrets
in the time to come

we go to bed
tired
depleted
of essential energy
but in a dream
our bodies fly
free
and feather-light
around the world

we hurdle
over rivers
move
soaring mountains
to distant countryside
without strain

yet in the morning
instead of feeling withered
like discarded
funeral flowers

we wake up fresh
filled with enthusiasm
transcending woes
of yesterday

*   *   *

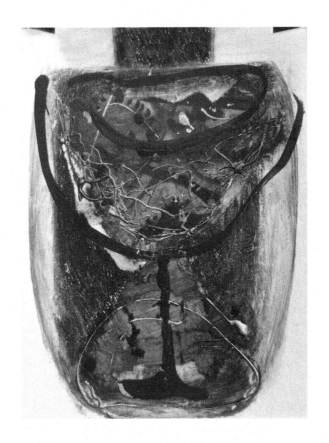

Jana Trnka, "Hoarfrost"

the breath of winter

hoarfrost
on morning windows
depicts
the fabulous scenes
created by the breath
of winter

a floral lace
trimming my gown
does not compare
with the beauty
of frozen panes

exotic palaces
tropical gardens
that will soon melt
in the rising sun

a fleeting mirage
of babylonian
hanging gardens
built by king
nebuchadnezzar
to sooth
the homesickness
of his beloved wife

*   *   *

dahlia

if there were a flower
that could compete
in a beauty contest
with the sovereign rose
—it is the dahlia

i speak to her
with fondness
giving her praise
for distinction
and charm

how wonderful
in the spring
to replant
her dormant tubers
and wait for them
to sprout
and profusely bloom
from midsummer
to the first frost

their starry petals
in an array of
shapes and colours
enchant the garden
as if by magic

*   *   *

ceremony of the dancing bees

fragrant nectar
bestowed free
by nature
from lavish countryside

according to myths
its potions
used to be remedy
for immortality
and eternal beauty
of ancient gods

gathered to beehives
from groves
and meadows
the ingredient
has to be changed
into honey
upon the ceremony
of dancing bees

set aside
for future use
an essential amount
is carefully filled
into hexagonal cells
of beeswax honeycombs

with the coming cold
a prudent voice of nature
urges the swarms

to remain
inside hives
nourished and sustained
for a winter

clung together
in clusters
the wintering bees
keep themselves
alive
until the burgeoning
spring

*   *   *

a journey throughout time

aging is a trip
on a trans-terrestrial train

it can go slow
or run too fast
from city
to a city
over wide territories
rivers and bridges
covering the distance
to the last station
of life

we are the passengers
viewing the world
behind windows
as it passes
in seconds
out of sight

for a lifetime journey
we get
a one-way ticket
valid from departure
to the terminal

and void!

*   *   *

Jana Trnka, *"The shift"*

the shift

if time is
another dimension
of the universe
everybody
at a point of dying
would be shifted
to another world

once
we had escaped
the terrestrial existence
we would rise
like the sacred phoenix
from the ashes
of his burning nest
resurrected
to another life

*   *   *

crossing a threshold

the greatest distance
everybody has to pass
occurs during dying

since no one has returned
to bring us memories
we know nothing
of the other side

that is
why we fear death
as a total loss
of our birthright
to an inherited world

yet
sometimes i remember
that death
has taken place
many times in my past
and as i crossed
his threshold
i set my foot
upon the path
to my true home

*   *   *

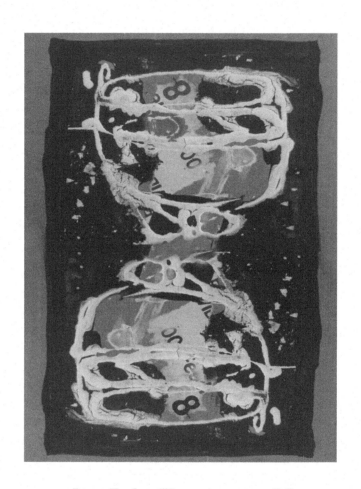

Jana Trnka, "Topsy turvy earth"

topsy turvy earth

the clouds hang low
opaque
and unfriendly
lacking warm kisses
of the sun

for several weeks
the entire earth
is topsy turvy
and people fear
the violent changes

volcanic eruptions
killing tsunamis
menacing earthquakes
tilting of earth-axis
natural disasters
reported daily
on the world news

the earth must be ill
people worry
while instinctive animals
look for new territories
before
the next catastrophe
strikes

*   *   *

boomers

in their extravagant lifestyle
they lost the ability
to express love
compassion
even in pain

they elected latest idols
fashionable
materialistic
dead
and created
a new
aaron's golden calf

a tireless robot
with
a mechanical heart
and an artificial brain

there is no god!
they insisted
in vain

but after
a horrific war
with the population
partially destroyed

their bygone compassion
for mankind
and a revival
of the denounced god
returned

with shame

*   *   *

unquiet past

Motto:

"Each face is its own landscape and is quietly vibrant with the invisible texture of memory, story, dream, need, want and gift that makes up the beauty of individual life."

J. O'Donohue

"There is a danger of losing touch with the past."

Sebastian Faulks

Jana Trnka, "Boy and the rose"

boy and the rose

a ballad

every spring
near the railway station
a wild rosebush comes
into full bloom

on the seventh of may
1945
defeated germany signed
an unconditional surrender
ending ww2
in suffering europe

after long struggles
new hopes and happiness
enticed a pair
of romantically attracted
teenagers
to a fragrant brier
for kissing
and making love

they did not notice
the perilous german squad
approaching
their defenceless city

despite a cease-fire
the arrogant ss soldiers
armed to the teeth
ruthlessly moved

toward
the railway station
ready to combat
the resistence force

as soon
as the boy apprehended
the imminent danger
he urged the girl deep
inside the bush
and kept his eyes
from the briar
on the marching troops

"halt!"
commanded
a reconnaissance-soldier
and frisking the boy
all over
found in his pocket
a dull
toyshop penknife
used by youths
for carving
their popular whistles
in the early spring

nine months later
the girl gave birth
to a baby boy
named

after his young father
unjustly executed
beside the bush
of a wild bleeding rose

*   *   *

icicle

in mid winter
our old garden pump
became entirely frozen

a tongue-piercing lick
of a crystal-clear icicle
hanging from the faucet
was a delicacy
i liked to share with
neighbourhood kids
for fun

but in no time
diphtheria
broke out among us
and with antibiotics
still unknown
many children
became affected with
the epidemic

confined to bed
i perceived a vision
of an ancient man
wheedling me slyly
to his shanty
where we used
to live together
in the distant past

but his ghostly visit
abruptly ended
when our family-doctor
cleared my throat
of the purulent mucous
choking me
to death

i sometimes recall
the mysterious visitor
whose intriguing appearance
still haunts me

*   *   *

the montblank fountain pen

it was a precious gift
perhaps stolen
from me
or mysteriously lost

the golden tip
of a fancy pen
produced
adroit effects
and ornamental tricks
on a flat page

like a fountain
spouting water
from a sacred well
the precise nib
of the magic pen
inked intuitively
my manuscript
with original themes

expressive words
brave opinions
moving across
the author's sky
as if with wings

the writer's freedom
to tell the truth
on poisonous pages
lost
and found facts

reverberations

of unjustly shed blood
and secret plots
reaching
to the convincing end

above all
my beloved pen
allowed me
to exchange letters
of forbidden love
within closed doors

until somebody
cut the story
short

*   *   *

Stania J. Slahor

the monument

after the communist coup
the six-hundred-year-old
augustinian monastery
in the moravian city
brno
was overtaken
by a new power
and purposely changed
into a university
student residence
to silence
its significance
for universal science

my assigned room
in a former monk's cell
was furnished coldly
with clumsy bunk beds
and propaganda posters
covering fine stucco
and religious murals
revered
and valued during
the monastic era

the sight of incivility
and rudeness
raised my inner protest
against such enormous
cultural loss

terrible sacrilege!
i cried in pain
grieving the destiny
of the country
i loved

by mere chance
another shocking event
took place inside
a monastery garden

looking
for a good spot
to study
in the late afternoon sun
i noticed
an oddly shaped bench
cut of sandstone
overgrown thickly
with weeds

examining it closely
i recognized
it to be a discarded
marble monument
of the 19th century genius
gregor mendel

as a monastery abbot
highly educated
in natural science

this meticulous scholar
used
this sun-facing garden
for planting rows
of fast-growing
pea plants

to study
a cross-pollination
he transferred
the tiny grains
of pea-pollen
from flower
to flower
with a fine brush

at a subsequent time
his attentive observation
and phenomenal
discovery
of the heredity pattern
became the basis
for the study
of modern genetics
recognized worldwide
to this day

iii

a century later
mendelian theories
were rejected
as ideologically
objectionable

by the stalinist hierarchy
in the soviet union
and by the entire east
communist block

as a consequence
the genetic techniques
of stalin's protegee
a scientific charlatan
trofim lysenko
using manipulation
and distortion
of the scientific process
caused serious
long-term harm
at the expense
of many human lives

as a matter of fact
lysenko never applied
actual science
but insisted
on the change in species
among the plants
through hybridization
and grafting

full of ambition
to convince stalin
of his ability
to increase
a poor soviet crop

lysenko glued
extra ears
to the natural
wheat stems

among others
he claimed
that the state
of being leafless
as a result
of having been plucked
could be inherited by
that organism's
descendants

iii

however
the modern science
emerging worldwide
out of studies
of genetic theories
made experimental verification
of ratios and heritability
discovered by mendel
much valid

iii

after the fall
of communism
during my visit
in brno

i found
that at one time
abandoned
mendel's monument
was masterly restored
and ceremonially moved
to the monastery courtyard

the sight
of his statue
overlooking
the famous garden
where his ingenious experiments
and discoveries
were accomplished
in the olden days

*   *   *

the family album

during
my european journeys
through old cities
i looked
for an ancient house
with a slated roof
verdigris eaves-troughs
grotesque gargoyles
inviting me home

my 'deja vu' feelings
were undoubtedly
attributed
to overheard stories
of my grandfather
a 1st world-war-casualty
whom i never met

his sepia photo
in our family album
shows
a handsome
middle-aged man
in an old-fashioned
austrian army uniform

his broad
bohemian face
with wide-set eyes
lacking any conceit
never faded
from my mind

that is why
to this day
i continue
to seek him inside
the deja-vu house
i imaginary built

*   *   *

Jana Trnka, "Beads"

mystery of beads

for hana again

the elaborate beads
handcrafted of seeds
slid on
a linen thread
inspired my teaching
in the drawing class

after school
alone in the art studio
i became lost
for a good two hours
in solitary thoughts
and sketching
till my daughter came
to bring me home
and the opening door
disturbed me
from a trance

seeing
my reluctance
to interrupt the work
the young girl
pronounced my drawing
just perfect

a year later
going through my portfolio
i found
the unfinished sketch

and recalled
the wonderful
mother-daughter empathy
at that time

twenty-three beads
on the neckless
tapering flawlessly on
a half-empty string

twenty-three beads
elaborately drawn
in minute detail
except the last
scarcely traced

my daughter's exact age
when she died

*   *   *

to visit
the terminally ill uncle
gave me
a wonderful lesson

the married couple
greeted each other
lovingly
driving away
imminent death

in their last
precious moments
shared together
my aunt pulled out
from her handbag
three red apples
her husband had gathered
from their orchard
before his illness
struck

recognizing the fruit
his deadly-white face
happily brightened
and deeply touched
he cried:
look at these apples
how nice!

my uncle
passed away
in the small hours
of the next morning

*   *   *

as poor as a church mouse

for my grandmother

my grandmother anna
a 1st world war widow
as poor
as a church mouse
reared her three
fatherless children
and bravely overcame
trauma of hardships

i like to recall
her cheap rented room
beside a cellar
where every article
had its mysterious past

lush asparagus
in the window
enhanced the interior
with the green shadows

a compact
corner kitchen
a wooden table
and benches
always clean
as a whistle

a blue-tiled stove
provided
a two-door oven
smelling heavenly
of home-baked bread

the entire room
in the 19th century
traditional style
aroused my interest
what were
its hidden secrets

a bad-omen-mirror
allegedly broken
when my grandpa
died
in a military hospital
on the albanian
front

a rococo music box
my grandparents'
wedding present
stubbornly mute
and never wound
since my grandpa's
draft

several books
some poetry
and fairy tales
i liked to illustrate
with the pastilles
tired of reading

the grandpa's empty bed
with straw-mattress
stuffed afresh
with the fragrance
of high summer

since
my grandmother
worked in the cinema
as an usher
she rather told me
thrilling
movie stories
instead of fairy tales

when i stayed
with her overnight
sleeping close
to the dark cellar
i became frightened
of evil ghosts
to interlope
and grab me

to set my mind
at rest
she brought to view
some family secrets

the best of all
that it was on my bed
where i came
into the world

afterwards
we prayed together
for my grandpa
relatives
and friends

alive or dead

*   *   *

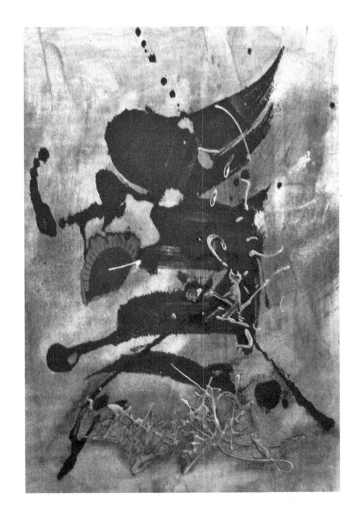

Jana Trnka, *"Barefoot on stubble"*

barefoot on stubble

the harvest was
threshed
reaped from
windswept fields
stacked
in barns

time for gleaners
to collect armfuls
of half empty ears
that provided them
a thrifty existence

i trailed
behind my grandma
in the ragged
farm-tracks
until she stopped
took off her shoes
and stepped
barefoot
on the stubble

i carefully
scrutinized her
picking up
scattered ears
into her oversize apron

well
i offered my help

but ouch!
bristly stubble
under bare soles
forced me nearly
to quit

how was it?
my grandma asked me
on the way home

and we both
laughed

*   *   *

an enduring dream

the tale with a hypothetical end

my uncle joseph
inherited
the ancestral manor
a centuries-old estate
decayed
and disintegrating
after long neglect
and violent
past events

the solitary settlement
on the bank of
a slow-moving river
spanned by a narrow
wooden bridge
outlived generations
who lacked all interest
in the modern world

but ambitious joseph
dreaming of restoring
family old glory
decided to build
a new mansion
by his own hands

from the forest
he cut loads of beams
for ceilings
sound and sweet-smelling
like his ancestral crib

in a desolate quarry
he dug big heaps
of yellow clay
used for pottery
in the past
and fired thousands
of bricks

it took him years
of hard work
to complete
his ambitious project

not long after he died
a dreadful flood
deluged the valley
washed away
the bridge
devastating
old holding

but by some mysterious fate
the infernal force
kept away
from the new structure
standing stationary
protected from wrath
by joseph's
enduring dream

*   *   *

the castles

the castles in the air
built of fantasy
desires and longing
are daydreamed
with open eyes

the fairytale castles
shaped
of pliable mud
by little children's hands
whose fragile walls
soon collapse
and evaporate
into clouds

the castle
built by my parents
when i was a child
never dwindled
from my mind

composed
of genuine articles
books and pictures
homemade toys
violin lectures
songs and poems
recited by heart

everything significant
for my journey
from innocence
to maturity
protecting me from
fruitless boredom
and harm

*   *   *

Jana Trnka, "Christmas"

secrets of christmas

to my parents

my father needed
a good two hours
for decorating
a fir tree
cut in the forest
before christmas

in a locked room
on a tablecloth
lay a set of plates
piled high with
gingerbread
shaped like fishes
hens and roosters
pigs for good luck
crescents and
hearts

all skilfully garnished
with white icing
chocolates and nuts
tied
to short loops
of strings

paraffin candles
phosphorous sparkles
glass ornaments
adorned with tinsels

and above all
a long-tail-star
soon thrust
to the treetop

there was not
enough room
in our house
for hiding secrets
with excited children
roaming and playing
everywhere

therefore
our mother
took us sledding
from a snow-covered hill
above the town

i remember
my wistful search
for angels
silently flying
across the sky
to our house
with plenty of presents
in their arms

yet on our return
my precious fantasy
of christmas
was forever lost

while at the door
shaking off snowflakes
from our winter coats
i caught a glimpse
of our father
behind the window
as he was clipping
a burning candle
to a top branch
of the fir

*   *   *

Stania J. Slahor

the shooting star

a charming formula

on a clear night
if you are
lucky enough
to set your eyes
upon a shooting star
utter a wish
on the brief sight
before it burns
and dies away
blind

your fervent longing
might be fulfilled
at once

*   *   *